Hooray for the Planet!
by Michael Fitzgerald

Illustrated by
John Burns

SPECIAL IDEAS

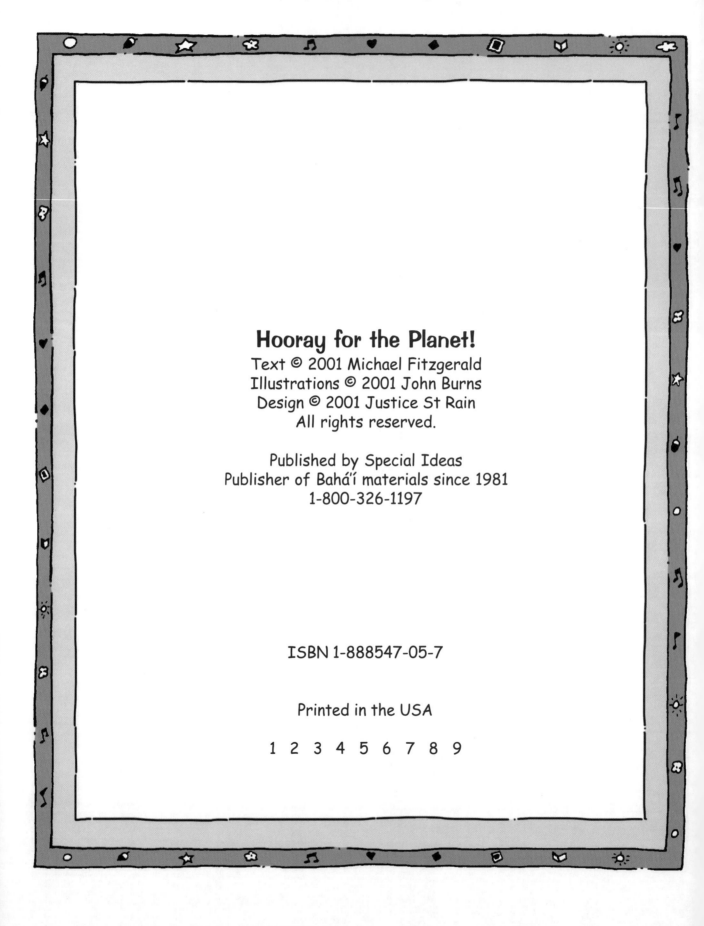

Hooray for the Planet!

Published by Special Ideas
Publisher of Bahá'í materials since 1981
1-800-326-1197

ISBN 1-888547-05-7

Printed in the USA

1 2 3 4 5 6 7 8 9

For my mother,
wonderful children's librarian,
composer of children's musicals,
and child at heart.

Michael

Hooray
for the planet!

Hooray
for the universe!

Hooray for trees!

Yippee for flowers!

Hooray
for the animals,
big and small!

Yea for deserts
and mountains
and plains
and valleys
and meadows
and islands!

Hooray for hugs
you can feel
in your toes!

Hooray
for Mom and Dad!

Hooray
for little gifts,
like a post-card...

or a phone call
from a friend...

or a
chunk of chocolate!

Let's hear it
for ethnic foods!

Ya-hoo for books!

Hooray
for ball games!

Ya-hoo for dancing!

Hooray for you!

Lets hear it for art!

Lets celebrate music.
All kinds!

Yippee for all races,
all backgrounds!

Hooray for all of us!

Yea for all religions!

Lets enjoy our
spiritual family.

Let's celebrate
churches
and mosques
and synagogues.

Let's celebrate
the
House of Worship.

Let's fill our lives
with
grateful prayer.

Praise be to God
for all
He has created!

Hooray
for no reason at all!

I'm so happy to
be a Bahá'í
because it leaves
room in my heart
for everyone.

Glorified art Thou, O Lord my God! I give Thee thanks inasmuch as Thou hast called me into being in Thy days, and infused into me Thy love and Thy knowledge. I beseech Thee, by Thy name whereby the goodly pearls of Thy wisdom and Thine utterance were brought forth out of the treasuries of the hearts of such of Thy servants as are nigh unto Thee, and through which the Day-Star of Thy name, the Compassionate, hath shed its radiance upon all that are in Thy heaven and on Thy earth, to supply me, by Thy grace and bounty, with Thy wondrous and hidden bounties.

These are the earliest days of my life, O my God, which Thou hast linked with Thine own days. Now that Thou hast conferred upon me so great an honor, withhold not from me the things Thou hast ordained for Thy chosen ones.

I am, O my God, but a tiny seed which Thou hast sown in the soil of Thy love, and caused to spring forth by the hand of Thy bounty. This seed craveth, therefore, in its inmost being, for the waters of Thy mercy and the living fountain of Thy grace. Send down upon it, from the heaven of Thy loving-kindness, that which will enable it to flourish beneath Thy shadow and within the borders of Thy court. Thou art He Who watereth the hearts of all that have recognized Thee from Thy plenteous stream and the fountain of Thy living waters.

Praised be God, the Lord of the worlds.

— Bahá'u'lláh

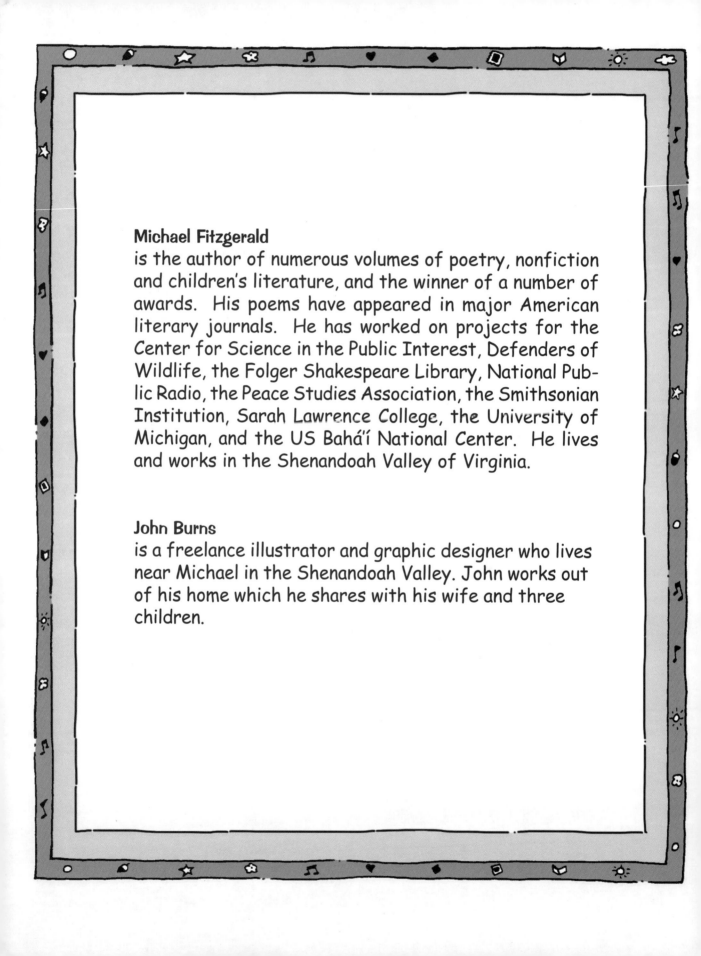

Michael Fitzgerald
is the author of numerous volumes of poetry, nonfiction and children's literature, and the winner of a number of awards. His poems have appeared in major American literary journals. He has worked on projects for the Center for Science in the Public Interest, Defenders of Wildlife, the Folger Shakespeare Library, National Public Radio, the Peace Studies Association, the Smithsonian Institution, Sarah Lawrence College, the University of Michigan, and the US Bahá'í National Center. He lives and works in the Shenandoah Valley of Virginia.

John Burns
is a freelance illustrator and graphic designer who lives near Michael in the Shenandoah Valley. John works out of his home which he shares with his wife and three children.